The Mummy Maker's Handbook

CONTENTS

Published by SCRIBO
25 Marlborough Place, Brighton BN1 1UB
A division of Book House, an imprint of
The Salariya Book Company Ltd
www.salariya.com
www.book-house.co.uk

SALARIYA

Printed and bound in China.
Printed on paper from sustainable sources.

PB ISBN-13: 978-1-910706-34-3

Created and designed by: David Salariya
Additional illustrators: Dave Antram, Nick Hewetson, John James
Editor: Jacqueline Ford
Editorial Assistant: Mark Williams

Visit our website at **www.book-house.co.uk**
or go to **www.salariya.com** for **free** electronic versions of:
You Wouldn't Want to be an Egyptian Mummy!
You Wouldn't Want to be a Roman Gladiator!
You Wouldn't Want to be a Polar Explorer!
You Wouldn't Want to sail on a 19th-Century Whaling Ship!

PAPER FROM
SUSTAINABLE
FORESTS

The Mummy Maker's Handbook

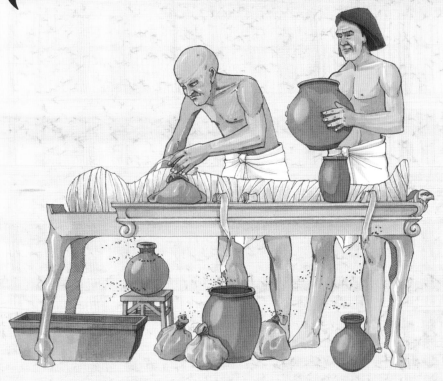

Jacqueline Morley
Illustrated by Mark Bergin

SCRIBO

INTRODUCTION

If you had been an ancient Egyptian living in Africa over 3,000 years ago, you would have been sure your homeland was favored by the gods. Each year you saw proof of this. Egypt was a desert land. It could grow nothing without the gods' help. Magically, every year, the gods caused the Nile River to overflow. This great river, that runs the length of Egypt, would flood its banks, leaving them covered with a thick layer of river mud. Egyptians rejoiced and thanked the gods. This mud was so rich and fertile that it grew crops big enough to feed everyone.

The Egyptian world

The Egyptians believed their country was the center of the world, and their king, or pharaoh, was a god. When he died he would join the sun god Ra, and travel with him through the sky. There were many legends about this journey. One said that the setting sun was swallowed by the sky goddess Nut, who was held aloft by her father Nu, god of the air, to separate her from her brother Geb, god of the earth.

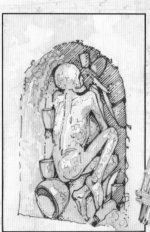

Egyptians buried people in the desert with objects they would need in the afterlife. In hot sand a body doesn't rot. It becomes a "mummy" —a preserved corpse.

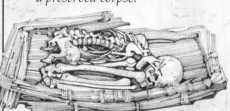

True or false?

The rise in the Nile is really caused by seasonal rain and melting snows, which occur much further south in Africa, near the river's source.

Answer on page 38.

There were farms all along the Nile, built on every scrap of fertile land. Many belonged to rich people. A rich family might have several large estates, and houses in the great cities whose glittering temples fronted the Nile. But most people lived in little mud-brick villages. Some earned a living by fishing or by making things to sell in their local market, but most were tenant farmers, who were given a patch of land of their own in return for working on their landlord's farm. These tenants were poor but they thanked the gods for giving them sunlight, water, and food.

There were no roads in the desert. The Nile was Egypt's great highway, busy with merchant ships, pleasure boats, and vessels carrying the pharaoh's officials on government business. In the distance on the western bank stand the thousand-year-old pyramid tombs of past pharaohs.

Pyramids

Reed boats

THE BEAUTIFUL WEST

Most people lived upon the east bank of the Nile but for burial they were taken to the western bank. Here, they began their journey to the Land of the Dead, which lay in the west, beyond the hills. The ancient Egyptians did not think of it as a gloomy place. The west was the direction in which the sun went down, and the sun was always born again the next day. Although "going into the west" meant dying, it also meant entering another, happier life, free from work or worry.

The priestess, Lady Henutmehyt, has just died. Her son gazes into the west, thinking of the journey he must help her make.

True or false?

Only very important people were allowed to put a pyramid on their tomb, like that on Lady Henutmehyt's.

Answer on page 38.

8

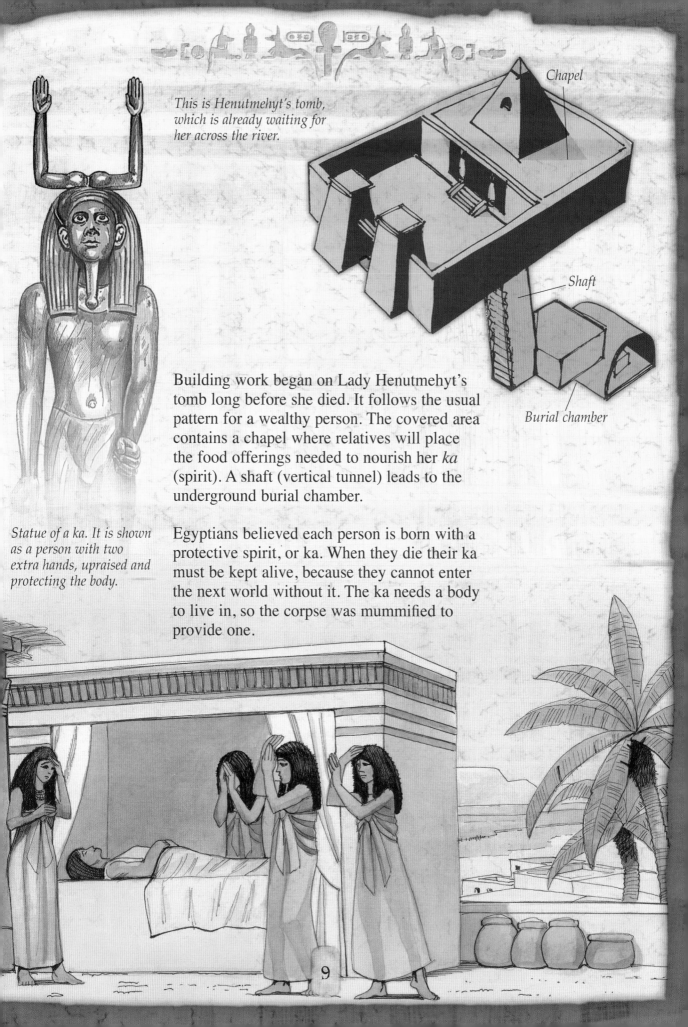

This is Henutmehyt's tomb, which is already waiting for her across the river.

Chapel

Shaft

Burial chamber

Statue of a ka. It is shown as a person with two extra hands, upraised and protecting the body.

Building work began on Lady Henutmehyt's tomb long before she died. It follows the usual pattern for a wealthy person. The covered area contains a chapel where relatives will place the food offerings needed to nourish her *ka* (spirit). A shaft (vertical tunnel) leads to the underground burial chamber.

Egyptians believed each person is born with a protective spirit, or ka. When they die their ka must be kept alive, because they cannot enter the next world without it. The ka needs a body to live in, so the corpse was mummified to provide one.

THE FIRST MUMMY

The story of their much-loved god Osiris was proof to all Egyptians that mummification was the way to eternal life. Legend told the Egyptians that in the days when the gods lived on earth, Osiris had been king of Egypt. His jealous brother Set murdered him and had his coffin flung into the Nile.

The river carried it to the sea, which swept it ashore near the city of Byblos in Syria. There, it settled against a tamarisk tree. Magically, the tree grew around the coffin and enclosed it in its trunk. It was such a fine trunk that the king of Byblos decided to make it into a pillar for his throne room.

How Set killed Osiris

At a palace feast, Set had produced a beautiful chest, saying it was a gift for anyone who could fit in it. Set urged Osiris to try, but when he got in, Set and his conspirators nailed down the lid.

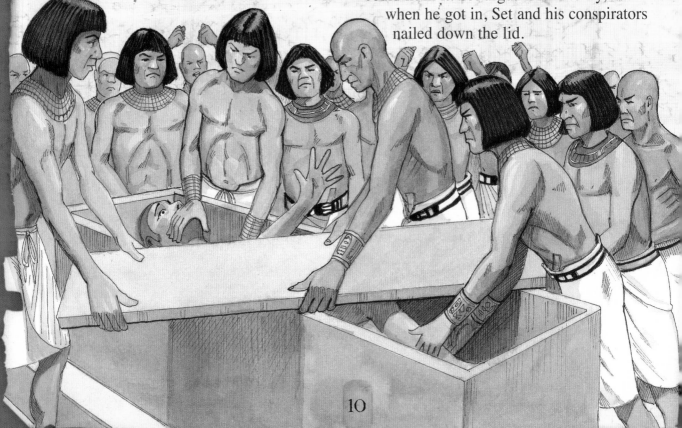

Isis searches for her murdered husband's body.

Osiris's faithful wife, the goddess Isis, spread her magical wings and flew up and down the world searching for the coffin that held Osiris's body. She learned that Osiris's coffin was inside the pillar and persuaded the king of Byblos to let her have it. When at last the precious coffin was hers, she brought it home to Egypt and hid it in the reeds of the Nile marshes. But Set went boar-hunting there one night and found it. He broke the coffin open, tore the body of Osiris into 14 pieces and scattered them the length of the land.

So, the weary Isis began her search again. She made a boat of papyrus reeds and travelled up and down the Nile until she had found every piece of her husband's body. She gathered them together and wept over them. Her cries were heard by Ra, the king of the gods, who sent the jackal-headed god Anubis to comfort her.

Osiris lives again

Anubis bound the pieces of Osiris's body together with linen bandages, wrapping them tightly round and round. Then Isis breathed into his mouth and he returned to life.

This, said the Egyptians, was how the first mummy was made. They spoke of a dead person as an "Osiris"—someone who is entering a new life.

Isis breathes life into Osiris's dead body.

11

ORDERING THE MUMMY

The men who prepare a body for the afterlife—embalmers—are members of an almost priest-like profession. They are responsible for everyone's safe journey to the next world, for they give the dead an everlasting body that can forever house their ka. The chief embalmer has the title "Master of Secrets"—because only he knows the secret treatments that preserve a corpse.

Lady Henutmehyt's son has come to the embalmers' showroom to select a suitable treatment for his mother's "Osiris." It must reflect her high position in life. As an important customer, Henutmehyt's son is received by the chief embalmer and shown models of various styles of mummy.

Wall painting

Before she died, Henutmehyt carefully chose the scenes that would be painted on the walls of her tomb. The ancient Egyptians believed that portraying an event could magically cause it to happen. So walls were normally painted with scenes of the dead person being mummified by Anubis or being welcomed into the next world by Osiris.

OUR MUMMY RANGE
to suit all budgets

Economy: Internal organs liquefied by cedar oil injections and drained away; full 40-day period in natron to ensure body is properly dessicated (dried out).

Mid-range: Internal organs removed manually and stored in jars; full drying period to be followed by oil-massage to repair shrivelling; complete bandaging and inclusion of amulets.

Luxury treatment: Anointing with scented oils, spices, milk, and wine, packing out of sunken areas, as well as restoration of lost hair and facial features, will ensure a completely lifelike Osiris. Funeral jewelry can be supplied as an optional extra.

A business receipt

This document, written on papyrus in demotic script (informal handwriting), is an embalmer's receipt of 270 BCE. It shows that the embalmer has received embalming materials and linen for the mummification of a corpse, and also promises that the mummy will be returned for burial on the 72nd day after the death.

PREVENTING DECAY

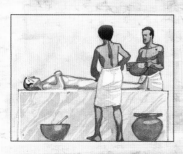

The first job of the embalmers is to prevent Henutmehyt's body from decaying. They wash it in water containing natron, a mild antiseptic (cleanser). The Egyptians believe water has life-giving properties, so the washing is also a sacred act symbolizing rebirth. The body is then transferred to an embalming table where the brain and internal organs are removed and the inside of the body is rinsed with palm wine. The purified body is packed around with natron crystals and left to dry out for 40 days.

What is natron?

Natron is a salt-like substance which absorbs moisture. Natron crystals occur naturally around the shores of certain Egyptian lakes.

Obsidian blade

A ritual knife with an obsidian blade is used to make a slit in the abdomen, on the left side. The lungs, liver, stomach, and intestines are removed through the slit.

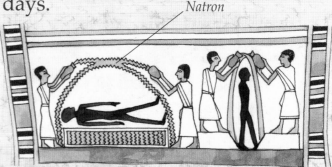

Natron

A painting on a coffin of around 600 BCE (above) shows embalmers purifying a body. They are pouring streams of natron solution over it from sacred vessels.

Attendant dressed as Anubis

In a scene from the same coffin (left), the body lies in a mound of natron on a lion-shaped embalming table. The leading attendant is portrayed as the god Anubis. This is probably the chief embalmer, wearing a mask to show his role as giver of new life.

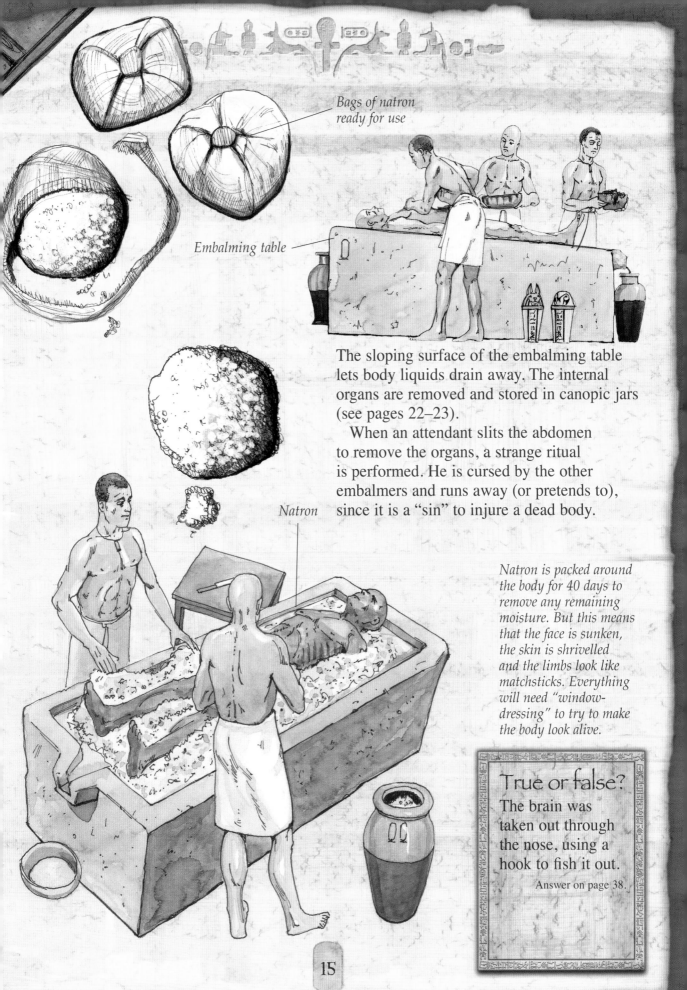

Bags of natron
ready for use

Embalming table

The sloping surface of the embalming table
lets body liquids drain away. The internal
organs are removed and stored in canopic jars
(see pages 22–23).

When an attendant slits the abdomen
to remove the organs, a strange ritual
is performed. He is cursed by the other
embalmers and runs away (or pretends to),
since it is a "sin" to injure a dead body.

Natron

*Natron is packed around
the body for 40 days to
remove any remaining
moisture. But this means
that the face is sunken,
the skin is shrivelled
and the limbs look like
matchsticks. Everything
will need "window-
dressing" to try to make
the body look alive.*

True or false?
The brain was
taken out through
the nose, using a
hook to fish it out.

Answer on page 38.

WRAPPING THE MUMMY

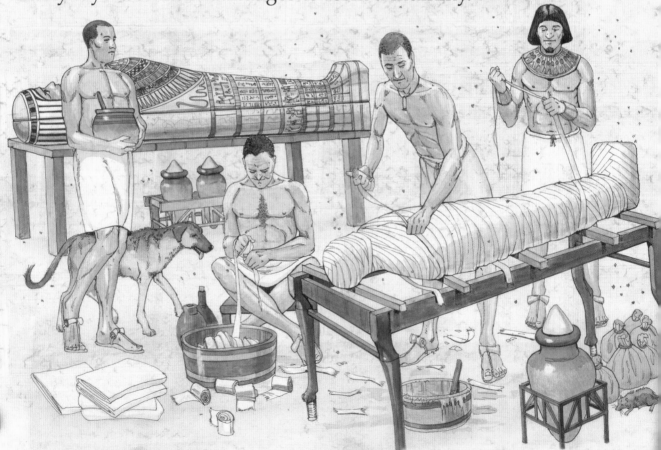

Henutmehyt's withered skin has been massaged with oil and her body packed with sawdust, packets of natron, and wads of linen, together with perfumes and cedar resin to give it a pleasant smell. Sunken areas of her face have been padded out; she has been given artificial eyes and her eyebrows have been repainted. She will now be wrapped in many layers of linen bandages to form a mummy.

Before wrapping begins, necklaces and pectorals (chest ornaments) bearing sacred emblems are hung around Henutmehyt's neck.

As the bandages are applied, magic amulets are bound between the layers. Molten resin is poured onto each layer as a preservative.

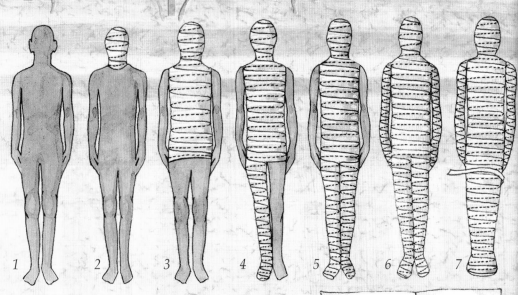

Wrapped up

How much linen went into wrapping a mummy? It varied and not always according to the dead person's importance. A minor official called Wah was wrapped in 375 square meters. That's a lot of linen!

1   2   3   4   5   6   7

Henutmehyt's reshaped body (1) was first wrapped around the head (2), then the torso (3). The legs were wrapped separately (4&5), then the arms (6), and then both legs together (7). Pads were added (8) and the mummy wrapped again (9), covered in a shroud (10), and tied with bands (11). A second shroud was added (12) and then tied (13).

8   9   10

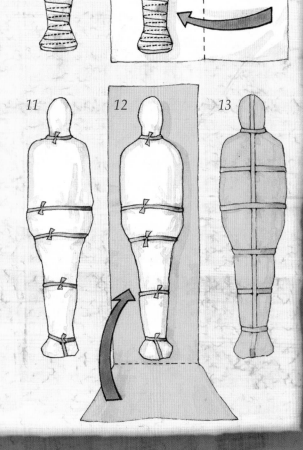

11   12   13

THE EMBALMER'S STOCKLIST

Natron: We hold large stocks of the purest kind.

Linen: We use only best-quality new linen, unlike cut-price embalmers who may include strips from cast-off garments or bed coverings.

Preservatives: We supply only the highest-quality beeswax, palm wine, juniper oil, incense, and cedar resin.

Cosmetic supplies: Our range includes linen pads, false hair, glass eyes, body paint, henna, and safflower dye.

Amulets: We stock every variety of charm, to ensure the safety of the Osiris on its journey to the next world.

MASKS AND COFFINS

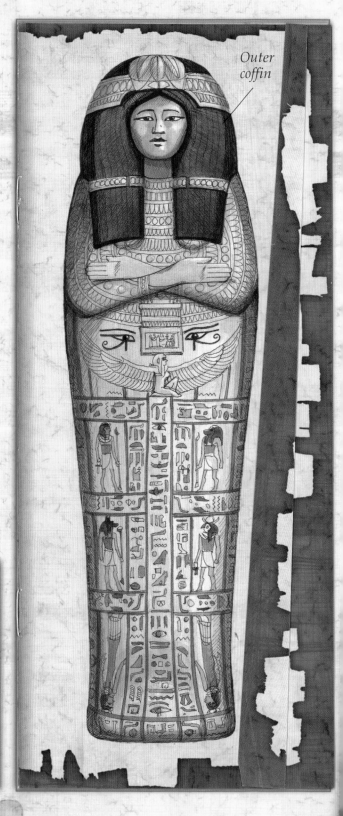

Outer coffin

Henutmehyt's finished mummy is now placed in its coffins. Her son has ordered two gilded coffins for her, to reflect her importance as a priestess. A royal person might have three. The coffins are set one inside the other. Both are in the form of a human being with crossed arms.

The human shape of the coffin is designed to protect Henutmehyt's spirit. Should anything disastrous happen to her mummy, the coffins will provide a substitute body for her ka.

True or false?

Mummies get their name from mummia, the Persian word for bitumen (a black, sticky liquid), because bitumen was used in mummification as a preservative.

Answer on page 38.

Henutmehyt is about to start a dangerous journey. The way to the next world is filled with evil spirits and she needs to know the right spells to fend them off. Fortunately The Book of the Dead contains spells which protect the newly dead. One of the most powerful is a spell to enable her to enter the boat of the sun god, Ra. It is written on a piece of papyrus and placed on her shroud, ready for when she needs it.

A priest dressed as Anubis recites spells over Henutmehyt's mummy.

Did you know?
Carrion beetles have been found in resin inside a coffin. They must have come from eggs laid in the corpse during embalming, which hatched while the resin was still soft.

FUNERAL CRAFTSMEN

T he embalmer was able to offer Henutmehyt's son a wide range of elaborate coffin designs made by skilful craftsmen. They have been trained in a tradition that goes back hundreds of centuries. The pharaohs have always demanded the highest standards of workmanship from these craftsmen, who make fine objects for the royal palaces and tombs.

These specialists also work for other wealthy clients. Their work follows long-established rules about the sort of decoration that will impress the gods.

Did you know?

Craftsmen were paid in goods: valuable things like jars of oil or rolls of expensive linen. Money had not yet been invented. Goods were bought and people were paid by exchanging things that both sides agreed to be of equal value.

A smooth surface is essential for gilding, so bare wood is coated with gesso (melted glue and chalk). The glue hardens as the gesso dries, providing a silky-smooth underlay for the gold.

A goldsmith beats a piece of gold into a very thin sheet.

Assistant making gesso

Goldsmith

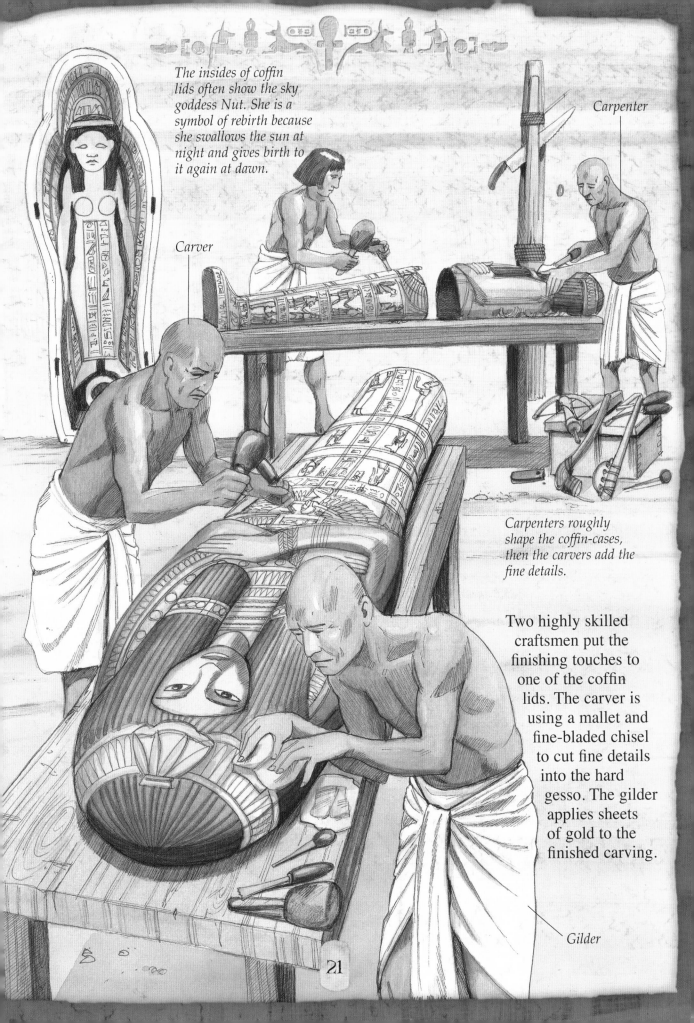

The insides of coffin lids often show the sky goddess Nut. She is a symbol of rebirth because she swallows the sun at night and gives birth to it again at dawn.

Carpenter

Carver

Carpenters roughly shape the coffin-cases, then the carvers add the fine details.

Two highly skilled craftsmen put the finishing touches to one of the coffin lids. The carver is using a mallet and fine-bladed chisel to cut fine details into the hard gesso. The gilder applies sheets of gold to the finished carving.

Gilder

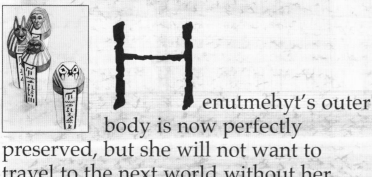

CANOPIC JARS

Henutmehyt's outer body is now perfectly preserved, but she will not want to travel to the next world without her insides. Removing them is one of the embalmers' first jobs, as otherwise they know the internal organs will rot very quickly and ruin the mummy. So, they are always preserved separately. The liver, lungs, stomach, and intestines have been dried in natron, anointed with scented oils, and coated with melted resin, before being linen-wrapped into four mini-mummies.

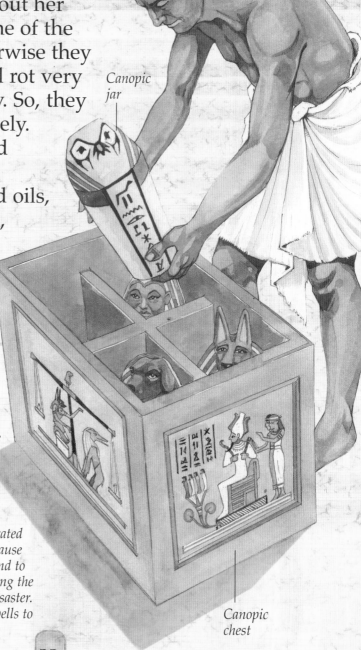

Canopic jar

Canopic chest

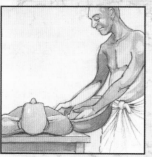

But what about the heart? That is the one organ that is left in the body. It is very important that it should not be separated from its owner, because the gods will demand to see it later. Mislaying the heart would be a disaster. There are special spells to guard against it.

Henutmehyt's canopic chest

Henutmehyt's canopic jars are made of painted wood. Each has a stopper of a different shape, to show what it contains.

The mummified organs are stored in four stoppered vessels known as canopic jars. They are kept in a special chest divided into four compartments, which will be placed in the tomb, close to the coffin. Henutmehyt's canopic chest is painted black.

The stoppers represent the four gods who protect the organs of the dead. The jackal-headed one guards the stomach, the human-headed one the liver, the falcon the intestines and the baboon the lungs.

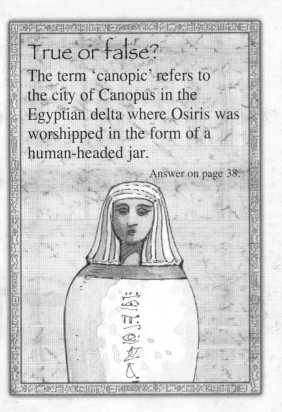

True or false?

The term 'canopic' refers to the city of Canopus in the Egyptian delta where Osiris was worshipped in the form of a human-headed jar.

Answer on page 38.

MAGIC

The ancient Egyptians have complete faith that magic can achieve things impossible to human beings, as long as it is done in exactly the right way. The right procedures are set out in the Book of the Dead, which lists the spells for each stage of mummification and the correct placing of bindings and amulets.

Did you know?
The Egyptians kept every body part they thought a person would need, but they did not bother with the brain. They thought it was just gunge and threw it away.

Lector-priest

When the chief embalmer puts on the mask of Anubis, the jackal-headed god, he acquires the gods' powers.

The chief embalmer is accompanied by an assistant known as a lector-priest, whose job it is to read out prayers. At appropriate moments in the ceremony, he chants spells to secure the protection of the gods and defeat evil spirits.

One of Henutmehyt's four painted wooden shabti boxes.

Model workers

Magic shabtis

For the purposes of magic, the representation of something as a drawing, a model, or in writing, is just as effective as the thing itself. So people are buried with models of things they will need in the afterlife. To ensure that they won't have to do any work in the next world, their tombs are stocked with little figures of servants who will work for them. These models, called *shabtis*, are packaged in special boxes.

The boxes hold 40 painted figures inscribed with spells to enable them to work for their owner.

Henutmehyt's son has ordered four magic bricks, each supporting an amulet. They will be set in her tomb, one by each wall, to ward off evil spirits coming from any direction—north, south, east or west.

The human figure guards the north wall.

The djed amulet guards the west wall.

The torch (a reed containing a wick) guards the south.

A clay Anubis figure guards the east.

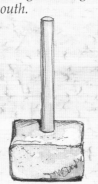

THE FUNERAL PROCESSION

The new, eternal body of Henutmehyt has been returned to her family. On the day of her funeral, a great procession sets out westward toward the Nile River. It is accompanying Henutmehyt on the first stage of her journey to a new life.

Her mummy rests on a canopied bier (platform) placed on a boat-shaped base. Bullocks are drawing the bier to the river on a sledge.

Chief priest

The chief priest heads the procession. He wears the leopard-skin robe of the priesthood of Amun, god of the city of Thebes.

ORDER OF SERVICE

Priests and family members will accompany the Osiris in procession to the riverside. Members of the public wishing to show their respect for the Lady Henutmehyt are invited to follow and join in the prayers and laments.

Boats will be waiting at the quayside for invited mourners to join in the sacred crossing of the river.

On the western bank the procession will continue to the tomb for the ritual of the Opening of the Mouth. After the sealing of the sarcophagus and tomb the ceremony will end with a celebratory meal.

The procession

More priests accompany the bier, burning incense and chanting spells. The chants mingle with the loud cries of women mourners, who beat their breasts and throw dust upon their heads as a sign of grief. Behind them come many servants carrying burial goods.

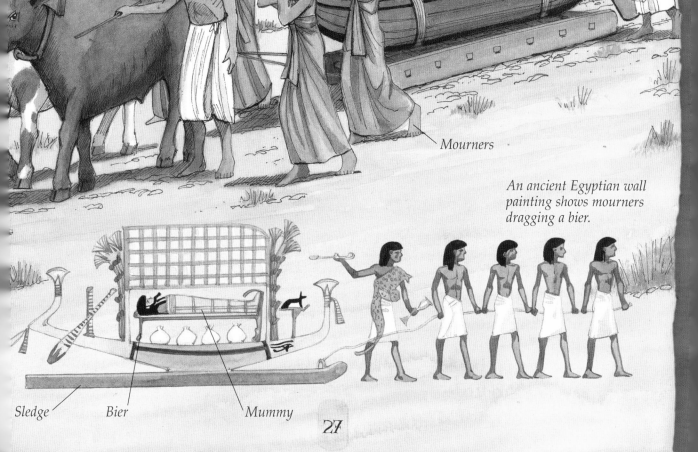

Mourners

An ancient Egyptian wall painting shows mourners dragging a bier.

Sledge   *Bier*   *Mummy*

The narrow shape of Egyptian boats evolved to navigate the Nile's swift currents. The tapered stern and sternpost were influenced by earlier boats made from bundles of papyrus.

Priest

Mummy

The priestess's body is taken for the last time across the Nile to the west bank, known as the Land of the Dead.

All Egyptians were buried in the west and had to make this sacred crossing. It recalled the voyage of the sun god who crossed the sky daily in a boat.

CROSSING THE RIVER

The washing and mummification of the priestess was carried out in the buildings attached to the temple prior to the day of her funeral procession.

Funeral procession

CROSSING THE RIVER

At the other end, the mummy in its coffin was carried along the causeway to its resting place by a procession of mourners and priests. The causeway was often completely enclosed to hide the coffin from view.

The body was symbolically
purified by priests to make it
fit to join the gods.

Mourner

Chief priest

Models of funeral boats were often put in tombs
in place of real ones. To ancient Egyptians,
a model or a picture of an object was just as
effective, for magic purposes, as the thing itself.

Attendants come to
meet the funeral boat
as it nears the shore.

Mourners

Once the ritual funeral boat
has been dragged down to the
river, it is then ferried across on
a larger boat, accompanied by
mourners and a priest.

The priestess's body is
transported to the landing stage
at the foot of the causeway that
leads to her final resting place.
It is then taken ashore.

After crossing the river, the procession brings Henutmehyt to her tomb, the "House of Eternity" which she has planned herself. Her mummy will rest below ground but her ka will rise up to the chapel to receive the food offerings placed there. The ka will magically eat the food, and as long as her ka is fed, Henutmehyt will live in the next world. Her family has a sacred duty to bring offerings to her forever.

The river crossing is like the sun's voyage into the west at nightfall. It leads to rebirth, in another day and another world.

While priests perform the last rituals, a funeral official oversees the bearers bringing Henutmehyt's furniture and household goods. He shows them where to place the goods in the burial chamber.

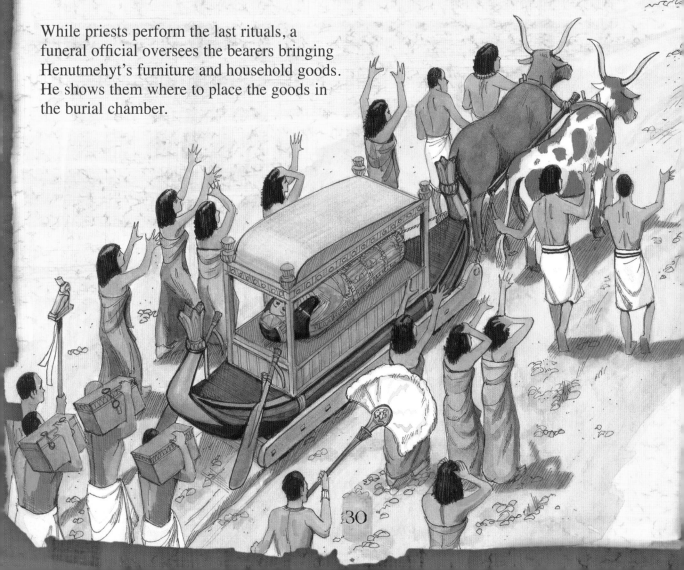

Osiris figures made of mud and barley are sometimes put in tombs. The grain will sprout, symbolising new life.

The chapel contains an image of Henutmehyt which the ka enters in order to feed.

Professional mourners

Though Henutmehyt's future is happy, loud weeping is essential to prove that the world misses her. Blue-robed, professional women mourners are hired to increase the laments.

OPENING OF THE MOUTH

The most important ceremony of all, the Opening of the Mouth, is held at the entrance to the tomb. Henutmehyt's mummy is set upright and purified with sprinklings of water and the burning of incense. Then the chief priest touches the mouth of the mummy-mask with ritual tools to bring Henutmehyt's senses to life again. Now that she can fully enjoy the afterlife, she is placed in her coffins in the burial chamber.

Mummified food

The goods placed in Henutmehyt's grave include a box of food containing four whole ducks and several joints of meat, each separately wrapped and mummified.

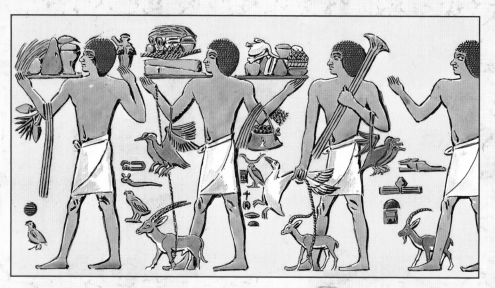

This tomb carving shows servants bearing food offerings for a ka. To ensure supplies will never fail, tombs are decorated with scenes of people bringing them.

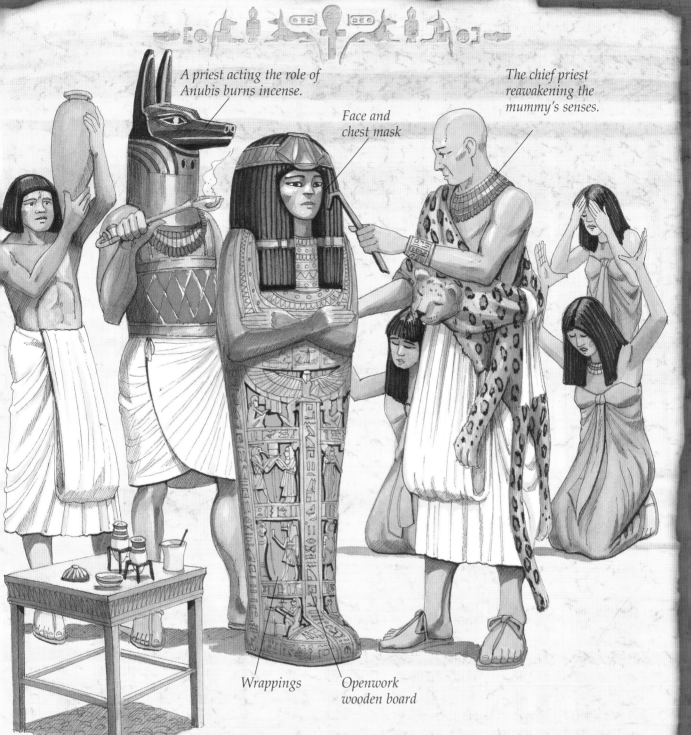

A priest acting the role of Anubis burns incense.

The chief priest reawakening the mummy's senses.

Face and chest mask

Wrappings

Openwork wooden board

Did you know?

Goods for the afterlife did not have to be new, or even usable. Flimsy dummy necklaces and sandals made of material too thin for walking have been found in tombs. They served as symbols of the real thing and were magically just as useful.

When the last family member has left the burial chamber, its floor is swept clean and its door is sealed forever.

IN THE AFTERLIFE

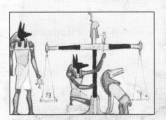

Thanks to the care her son has taken over her funeral, Henutmehyt has reached the judgement hall of Osiris, lord of the dead. She has had to pass through many fiery gateways, whose guardians turn away anyone who fails to recite the correct spells. Now she faces the worst ordeal of all, the weighing of her heart in the Scales of Truth. Math, the goddess of truth, stands watching as Anubis adjusts the balance and Thoth, god of knowledge, records the result. A monster waits nearby to gobble heavy hearts.

True or false?

The person who paid the expenses of a funeral was entitled to inherit the dead person's estate.

Answer on page 38.

A spell from the Book of the Dead:
O my heart!
Do not stand up as witness against me!
Do not be opposed to me in the tribunal.
Do not be hostile to me in the presence of the Keeper of the Balance!

Math

Monster

Thoth

Anubis

Ancient Egyptian painting of the weighing of the heart.

Those who are judged to have lived well are welcomed by Osiris to the Field of Reeds, a happy world where the corn grows tall.

It is a place very like the world of the living but free from care. Shabti servants will come to life to do the hard work.

The scenes painted on the walls of tombs will become reality. A favorite scene shows the dead feasting beneath a sacred tree.

Henutmehyt awaits the verdict.
Bad deeds make a heart heavy.
If her heart is no heavier than the
Feather of Truth, all will be well.

TOMB ROBBERS

Henutmehyt rests peacefully in her tomb, but for how long? She is quite likely to be disturbed by tomb robbers breaking in to steal the valuable objects buried with her, such as gem-encrusted jewelry, precious perfumed oils, and expensive linen.

Pharaoh's official

Tomb robbers

An official is arresting suspected tomb robbers. If found guilty they face death by impalement on a spike.

The enormous riches buried with the pharaohs are the thieves' prime target, but most tombs are robbed. Where there are no signs of a break-in, the undertakers may have been the culprits. One "perfect" mummy was found to have the imprints of missing jewelry in the resin between its bandages when it was unwrapped. It must have been robbed during the embalming!

NEW USES FOR OLD MUMMIES:

1. **Ailments:** Medieval doctors prescribed powdered mummy to cure almost everything! Huge quantities were exported to Europe to be sold and swallowed, until well into the 17th century.
2. **Handy torches:** Mummy arms and legs were set alight.
3. **Ballast:** Used to steady ships bound for Europe.
4. **Paint coloring:** For the color known as "mummy brown."
5 **Firewood:** Mummies were used as an extra source of fuel.
6. **Entertainment:** Public unwrapping was very popular in 19th-century England.

GLOSSARY

amulet a charm or piece of jewelry thought to have magical protective properties.

ballast any heavy material placed in the hold (bottom) of a ship to make it low enough in the water not to capsize.

beeswax wax produced by bees, with which they build the cells of their hives.

bier a movable stand on which a coffin is placed before burial.

bitumen a tar-like substance.

carrion beetles beetles that feed on dead bodies.

cholera an often fatal infection that can be caught from contaminated food or water.

demotic script a simplified form of ancient Egyptian writing, which was quicker to write than the hieroglyphic alphabet.

dessicated dried out.

dismembered with body parts chopped into pieces.

embalmer a person whose trade is the preserving of bodies before burial.

gilded covered with a thin sheet of beaten gold.

henna powder made from the leaves of a tropical plant, which produces a reddish-brown stain.

ibis a wading bird with a long curved beak, related to the heron.

impalement being stuck on a sharp spike (resulting in death, if intended as a punishment).

incense a mixture of gums and spices used to produce a sweet smell when burned.

ka a person's protective spirit.

lament an expression of grief.

natron a natural form of salt.

obsidian a glass-like volcanic rock which splinters into sharp pieces.

openwork decoration with a pattern of holes.

papyrus a reed growing beside the Nile, used by the ancient Egyptians to make paper.

resin a gummy substance produced by certain trees, which hardens as it dries.

ritual an act which has a special meaning, usually religious.

safflower a yellow-flowered thistle-like plant, which produces red and yellow dyes.

sarcophagus a stone coffin.

shroud a cloth in which a corpse is wrapped for burial.

Thebes formerly ancient Egypt's capital city, though by Henutmehyt's day the capital had been moved to the north.

Answers

Page 6: TRUE. Rain and melting snow come from the Ethiopian highlands, a vast mountain area stretching into Ethiopia, Eritrea, and northern Somalia.

Page 8: FALSE. Pyramids originally marked only royal tombs. By the time of Henutmehyt's death (around 1250 BCE), it was quite usual to put a small pyramid on a tomb.

Page 15: TRUE. The brain was not considered important and was thrown away.

Page 18: TRUE AND FALSE! Mummies were so named in medieval times. People thought the hardened black substance that had been poured over them was bitumen. They were mistaken. It was resin.

Page 23: TRUE. Past scholars wrongly thought the stoppered burial jars represented the Canopus god, and the term has stuck.

Page 34: TRUE. In practice, the dead person's closest relative normally paid.

INDEX